Places We Live

Living Beside the Ocean

Ellen Labrecque

heinemann
raintree

To contact Capstone Global Library, please call 800-747-4992, or visit our web site www.capstonepub.com

Edited by James Benefield and Brenda Haugen
Designed by Richard Parker
Original illustrations © Capstone Global Library Ltd
Picture research by Jo Miller
Production by Helen McCreath
Originated by Capstone Global Library Ltd
Printed and bound in China by Leo Paper Group

18 17 16 15 14
10 9 8 7 6 5 4 3 2 1

Library of Congress Cataloging-in-Publication Data
Labrecque, Ellen.
  Living beside the sea / Ellen Labrecque.
    pages cm.—(Places we live)
  Includes bibliographical references and index.
  ISBN 978-1-4846-0803-6 (hb)—ISBN 978-1-4846-0810-4 (pb)—ISBN 978-1-4846-0824-1 (ebook) 1. Ocean—Juvenile literature. 2. Seas—Juvenile literature. 3. Seashore—Juvenile literature. I. Title.
  GF65.L335 2015
  304.20914'6—dc23   2014013629

This book has been officially leveled by using the F&P Text Level Gradient™ Leveling System.

Acknowledgments
We would like to thank the following for permission to reproduce the following photographs: Alamy: Bjarki Reyr MR, 20, Geof Kirby, 12, JB-2078, 8, Mark Conlin, 21, USA, 11; Dreamstime: Thomas Perkins, 5; Newscom: Getty Images/AFP/Gregory Boissy, 23, Hindustan Times, 27, Michael Weber Image Broker, 17, Robert Harding/Purcell-Holmes, 22, Robert Harding/Tony Waltham, 16, Steve Smith Stock Connection Worldwide, 14, ZUMA Press/Koichiri Tezuka-Mainichi Shimbun, 15; Shutterstock: gary yim, 25, Marek Stefunko, 19, nui7711, 26, oksana perkins, 7, Paul J Martin, 10, Razvy, 9, spirit of america, 18, trubavin, 4, WAMVD, cover, wdeon, 24; Superstock: age fotostock/Martin Zwick, 13.

Design Elements: Shutterstock: donatas1205, Olympus.

We would like to thank Rachel Bowles for her invaluable help in the preparation of this book.

Contents

Some words are shown in bold, **like this**. You can find out what they mean by looking in the glossary.

What Is the Ocean?

Seas are giant areas of salty water. The biggest seas are called oceans. They are one of the most important places people find food. They also provide **minerals**, oil, and natural gas from their seabeds.

Some beaches are flat and sandy.

Some beaches can have lots of rocks and pebbles on them. You can still have fun there, though!

Seas and oceans are home to a huge number of plants and animals—even more than live on dry land. It's a good place for people to live, too. The water absorbs the sun's heat, so that people and the whole planet don't get too hot.

Where Are Oceans?

Oceans and seas cover over 70 percent of the world's surface. The world's seas and oceans don't have borders. Water flows between them. We have different names for different parts of seas and oceans.

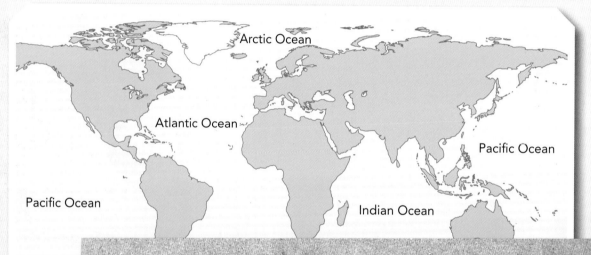

Earth's major oceans, listed by size

1. Pacific Ocean, 63.8 million square miles (about 165 million square kilometers)

2. Atlantic Ocean, about 41 million square miles (about 106,460,000 square kilometers)

3. Indian Ocean, about 28 million square miles (about 73,440,000 square kilometers)

The Pacific Ocean is the biggest ocean on Earth. It covers one-third of the world's surface. It stretches from Antarctica almost up to the Arctic Circle. Many people around the world live near the Pacific Ocean.

Living by the Ocean

People all over the world live in **settlements** by seas and oceans. Some people live in these homes all year around. Other people own homes here, but live and work inland.

People live and relax by oceans and seas.

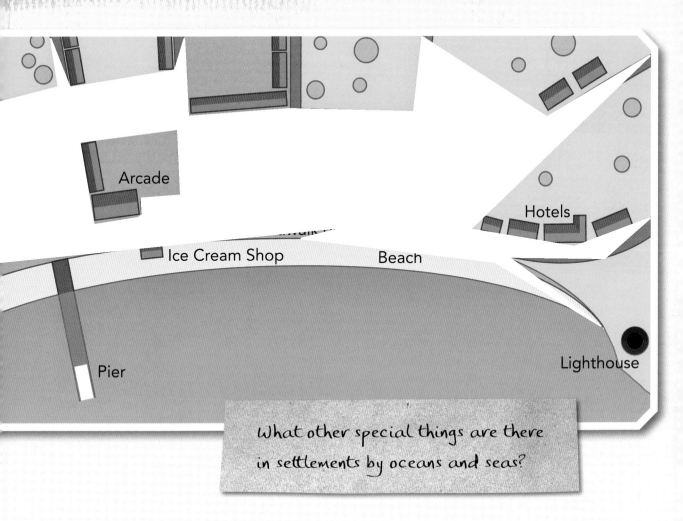

Arcade

Ice Cream Shop

Beach

Hotels

Pier

Lighthouse

What other special things are there in settlements by oceans and seas?

Seaside settlements have many things in common with other types of settlement. For example, they have stores and houses. But they also might have special things such as a lighthouse. This is a tall building with a large light that warns ships that there are nearby rocks.

Living by the Ocean in the Past

Fishing **communities** have always lived by seas and oceans. But only rich people went on holiday there. Poor people didn't have enough money to travel to the seaside. This all changed when railroads were built in the 1800s.

Trains made traveling to the beach much cheaper.

In 1870, a boardwalk was built in Atlantic City, New Jersey.

As more people came to seas and oceans, the area became built up. Many more homes, stores, and restaurants were built. People can walk along the **piers** and **boardwalks**.

City Living by the Ocean

Many people live in cities by seas and oceans. Cities grew up there as the water helped people **trade** with other places. They could easily sail in and out with the things they were trading.

Cape Town, South Africa, has a busy **port**. The city is where the Atlantic and Indian oceans meet.

Aberdeen, Scotland, sits on the North Sea, where a lot of oil drilling takes place.

Some cities have grown up by seas and oceans because of oil. Most people who work on **oil rigs** live by the water. People on rigs help dig for oil that is far below seas and oceans and deep into the seabed.

Wild Weather

Living by water can be dangerous. During storms, seas and oceans can flood the land and can destroy buildings and hurt people. People in some towns have built beach houses on stilts to protect houses from floods.

Seawalls are built to stop water from flooding **settlements**.

Tsunami waters can be up to
100 feet (30 meters) high.

Tsunamis are especially dangerous. They are
a series of waves that send lots of water onto
the land. Underwater earthquakes can cause
them. A tsunami hit Japan in 2011 killing as
many as 18,000 people.

Safe from the Water?

Coastal **erosion** is a danger for **communities** who live by seas and oceans. This is when the land and beach are worn away by waves, winds, and **tides**. The land can take homes and buildings with it.

The Holderness Coastline in the United Kingdom is one of the fastest-eroding coastlines in Europe.

Adding sand to a beach can prevent erosion.

Luckily, there are ways to slow down erosion. One way is to put up barriers. This stops waves from hitting the sand and eroding it. Sand and boulders can also be brought in to help build up beaches.

Getting Around

You can get to most places by the ocean and sea by road. **Tourists** travel on cruise ships to see different things. People even cruise to the coasts of Antarctica, even though there are no towns there!

Antarctica has no towns, but there are lots of penguins!

The Bajau live in raised houses or on boats.

The Bajau people in Southeast Asia, on the Pacific Ocean, don't just travel on boats. Some live in houseboats. Others live in stilt houses. They say that when they spend a night on land they feel land sick, not seasick.

What Is School Like?

Most children who live by oceans and seas go to schools just like you. Some children living in very small **communities** stay at home and their parents teach them. Others go away to boarding school, if no schools are nearby.

Inuit communities in Greenland sometimes send children far away to school.

Students who live near seas and oceans learn about what life is like on a boat.

Some students don't just learn about the water—they go to school on it! Programs such as Ocean Classroom and Semester at Sea teach students while they are on boats.

Where Do People Work?

People can have regular jobs such as doctors and teachers and live by seas and oceans. However, there are jobs found just here. There are fishermen and beach lifeguards.

Coast guards protect people in boats out in the water. Lifeguards keep people safe on the beach.

Laird Hamilton lives in Hawaii and surfs waves that are 100 feet (30 meters) high.

Some people who live in beach towns work in jobs that serve **tourists**. For example, they work in hotels or restaurants. Some people who live in beach towns surf for a living.

Fun Things to Do

Some people love to visit places by seas and oceans. They can swim, explore the water, and play on the beach. People sunbathe and play sports on most kinds of beaches. If the beach is sandy, people can build sand castles.

Volleyball is a great beach sport.

Peggy's Cove in Nova Scotia, Canada, is a great rocky beach to explore. You can find lots of things in rock pools.

If you like adventure, rocky beaches offer great places to explore. If it's too rocky, you can get in a boat. You could search for wildlife, from dolphins to sea turtles, swimming in the waters.

Living by Water in the Future

Some scientists believe living by water is getting harder because of **climate change**. Sea levels are rising as ice and **glaciers** melt. This could cause flooding, which can destroy seaside homes. There is also water **pollution**.

Water pollution kills plant and animal life.

In some places, people organize outings to pick up beach litter.

Work is being done to clean up seas and oceans. In some places, rules have been set to stop people from dumping trash into the sea. Groups such as Oceana help to teach people how to protect areas near seas and oceans.

Fun Facts

- People who study oceans are called oceanographers.

- Nearly 2.4 billion people in the world live within 60 miles (100 kilometers) of seas and oceans.

- World Oceans Day is celebrated every year on June 8.

- The largest animal in the ocean is the blue whale.

- During the winter, the Arctic Ocean is almost completely covered in ice.

- Some studies tell us that people who live by seas and oceans are happier than those who live inland!

Quiz

Which of the following sentences are true? Which are false?

1. There is more land than water on Earth.

2. The biggest ocean in the world is the Arctic.

3. Underwater earthquakes can cause tsunamis.

4. Erosion is not dangerous.

5. Sea and ocean levels are going down.

5. False. Some scientists think that levels are rising because of climate change.

4. False. Eorsion can destroy people's homes.

3. True.

2. False. The world's biggest ocean is the Pacific.

1. False. The oceans and seas cover about 72 percent of Earth's surface.

Glossary

boardwalk wooden walkway by the sea, across sand, where people like to stroll

climate change change in weather patterns or the planet's temperature over many years

community group of people or animals who share the same things, such as where they live

erosion when land or rock has been worn or ground down over time by water, ice, snow, or wind

glacier huge river of ice or iceberg. You can find these near and in the Arctic or the Antarctic.

mineral special substance from rocks that can be found in the sea—for example, salt

oil rig large, raised platform out in the sea. People work on these to drill oil from below the seabed.

pier raised walkway from land out over water

pollution when harmful substances are released into the sea, air, or ground. This can hurt or kill animals, plants, and even people.

port where boats load or unload what they carry

settlement place where people live, such as a village, town, or city

tide regular rise and fall of the height of the sea

tourist person who visits another place for fun

trade when you buy or sell things

Find Out More

Books

Arnosky, Jim. *Beachcombing: Exploring the Seashore.*
New York: Penguin, 2014.

Parker, Steve. *100 Things You Should Know About the
Seashore.* Broomall, Pa.: Mason Crest, 2011.

Rivera, Sheila. *Ocean* (First Step Nonfiction). Minneapolis:
Lerner, 2005.

Internet sites

Facthound offers a safe, fun way to find Internet sites
related to this book. All of the sites on Facthound have
been researched by our staff.

Here's all you do:

Visit www.facthound.com

Type in this code: 9781484608036

Index